Contents of a Minute

LAST POEMS

Josephine Jacobsen

EDITED BY

Elizabeth Spires

Sarabande  Books

LOUISVILLE, KENTUCKY

© 2008 by The Estate of Josephine Jacobsen

FIRST EDITION

Managing Editor
Sarabande Books, Inc.
2234 Dundee Road, Suite 200
Louisville, KY 40205

Library of Congress Cataloging-in-Publication Data

Jacobsen, Josephine.
  Contents of a minute : last poems / by Josephine Jacobsen. — 1st ed.
    p. cm. — (Quarternote chapbook series ; #7)
  Includes bibliographical references and index.
  ISBN 978-1-932511-58-1 (pbk. : alk. paper)
  I. Title.

PS3519.A424C66 2008
811'.54—dc22

                      2007021779

Cover and text design by Kirkby Gann Tittle.

Manufactured in Canada.
This book is printed on acid-free paper.

Sarabande Books is a nonprofit literary organization.

This project is supported in part by an award from the National Endowment for the Arts.

The Kentucky Arts Council, a state agency in the Commerce Cabinet, provides operational support funding for Sarabande Books with state tax dollars and federal funding from the National Endowment for the Arts, which believes that a great nation deserves great art.

Contents

Acknowledgments

Grateful acknowledgment is made to the editors of the following magazines where many of these poems first appeared:

Atlanta Review: "Piazza di Spagna"

Commonweal: "Manny in the Wasps' Nest"

Five Points: "Purgatory is Nearer in November"; "Natural"; "Obscurity;" "Recruit, on the Hill"

Gettysburg Review: "Boy and Girl in November"; "Parrot"

Image: "Stroke"

The New Criterion: "Color Song"

The New Yorker: "The Apprentice"; "The Companions"; "Contents of a Minute"; "Distinctions"; "Old Mr. Forrester"; "Program"; "Voyage"

Ploughshares: "A Blessing"; "Obit"

Poetry: "The Ugly Old Lady"

Poetry Speaks Calendar 2008: "Boy and Girl in November"; "Parrot"

The Potomac Review: "Last Will and Testament"

Introduction

In 1995, at the age of eighty-seven, Josephine Jacobsen published her last full-length collection of poetry, *In the Crevice of Time: New and Collected Poems* (Johns Hopkins Press). With some difficulty—her eyesight was failing, and she could no longer type nor easily hold a pen—she continued to write a poem or two a year for the next several years. (Her last poem, "The Companions," came to her in a dream and was dictated to her friend and secretary Charlotte Blaylock one morning.) When death finally overtook her in 2003, she left a handful of uncollected poems, including seven that had appeared in *The New Yorker*.

It was a precious sheaf, admittedly too thin to publish as a book, though as her friend and one-time editor (I had helped her put together her book of occasional prose, *The Instant of Knowing*, in 1996), I hoped that one day that handful of poems would come together in a final form.

And then, as fate or luck would have it, a box of her personal memorabilia and manuscripts turned up at an auction. The box contained family photos, personal letters, cancelled checks, and short stories and poems dating from the 1930s to the early 1940s. When I was offered the chance to read the poems in that box by the purchaser, I found seven poems, not included in any of her early books, that were of a high enough literary caliber to be part of her permanent oeuvre.

The contents of this chapbook then, bringing together as it does Jacobsen's last poems and lost poems, spans not a minute but a lifetime.

Elizabeth Spires

A Blessing

I rejoice in the poems not written:
the cruelly discarded: the crippled,
the asthmatic, the anemic: the poem

about a photograph: about what love
is like: about how strangely I
felt that day: about something about me,

noticed. Bless you, go on the ash-heap,
that fine compost from muscle, blood, bone,
which fuels surely the green slick stalk.

(MacDowell Colony, June 18th, 1983)

The Apprentice

When she was five
after her radiant mother
kissed her and vanished to unimaginable
adult delights, the last, last thing she saw
each night was her nurse's black, beloved face,
lit in the open doorway to night, angel
of the portal. If she had been bad,
let alone unrepentant, the ritual words
Alice had taught her were withheld, the token
for sleep, the dark's blessing: "Sweet dreams."
"No, no! Sweet dreams!" "Good night," said Alice,
creature of the light, implacable and just.
Panic pushed out tears. "No, no. Sweet *dreams!*"
And finally, in dignified mercy, "Sweet dreams," said Alice.
Sleep took the bed. So, early
and inadvertently, she learned words'

brute magic.

Distinctions

It is hard to love the pessimist
holding forth from his dank ditch
searching for woes as for Easter eggs
like Proust's butler.

It is hard to love the optimist
putting his jolly mask on grief,
predicting joys which never come
but will be said to have done so.

It is easy to love the feckless one
who takes the days' jerky ride
without the help of theory,
constantly thrown by chance,

surprised by joy, surprised by woe.
A constant wonderer who never
triumphed in foresight—
innocently astonished.

Piazza di Spagna

Estragon says to Vladimir
(or vice versa) of happiness
recollected in distress: how
unpleasant that must be.

Ah Estragon, ah Vladimir,
discussing loss, the poet's
mother-lode. On the Spanish Steps
chill fingers the bone.

As the sun drops and drops,
stare across at the small,
cold, invisible room
where loss has reveled;

where loss's aficionado
labored to grasp and hold
a green felicity,
Apollo's summer look.

Loss has its *son et lumière*
to show what it has got
and means to keep: a hundred poems,
bright blood, a girl.

Program

The glass in her hand flares
like a flower. It is cold and clear
and has a slender long stem.

Over the Martini she sees things
just happened. Her grandmother
saw two dead men, husband

and father, though she saw
elaborate coffins. Here the dead
arrive at six o'clock.

They lie in the street
in artless attitudes.
No pan-in to see

if the eyes are closed or not.
Obviously her Martini is blameless,
and she takes small sips,

with a slight shudder, from the chill
of glass, or scene, or both.
From a new angle still they lie.

She is aware of a deeper dismay.
She feels a cold horny finger—
habit's—gently touch her heart.

She is positive it is happening,
and stares harder at the shapes, but they are gone.
And someone is talking weather.

The Ugly Old Lady

her hair in metal rows
under a roaring cone
is modesty itself,

aspires in all humility
just to the diminution
of her ugliness.

She has the secret humble wish
not to detract from all the sum
of a rare trust

she knows exists elsewhere:
the thing that Helen's glass
took and gave back,

that lifted from some sea
stern Aphrodite
on her brittle shell.

Contents of a Minute

The woman across the hall
is dying. She talks herself into death
with a low rapid jumble.
A rich African voice is talking
over hers. It speaks of *green*,
as in *pastures*; *still*, as in *waters*.
A high clamor of geese falls
through the dusk, taking a flock south.
Geese are gone. And the woman.
Elsewhere, the wind
blows in from left field.

Stroke

In the dark, clearly, *One!* says the clock.
In the dark, the waker hears the stroke.
Has a day dropped forever
into the insatiable maw which stalks
the hour and cannot be satisfied?
Or is the new inscrutable day,
uninstructed in guarantees, present?

Silence leaves the waker awake
minus identity or anchor
staring through time's flimsy count
to *now. Now* brings up its denizens
of the past, beloved and implacable.
Sleep will not pass its fingers
over the waker's lids until a stroke
snatches him in time.

Last Will and Testament

At the lowest points, he went
into a restaurant (maybe three a night)
and took a menu to study;

pocketed half a dozen cubes
of sugar, drank good cold water, ate,
if there was one, a roll,

found the menu flat
and unprofitable, left, between
busboy and waiter.

Repetition impossible;
but lots of restaurants in winter
Manhattan.

The odd reading, or loan, or donkey work
helped. Writing, he chose and chose.
He wrote good poetry.

He wrote honed out-of-season
lyrics. Some got printed
and achieved a mini-reputation.

He wrote lines better than good
and one monosyllabic
indestructible phrase

that can't wear or fade or chip.
I can't remember the title
of the poem it came from.

Six monosyllables. Enough.
My copy slipped away;
it was a paperback

of which I had five copies.
They all went somewhere before,
or after, he died.

He gave a small reading
in a formal house:
receptive people.

Too long, after the reading,
he said and drank too much. The hostess
rose to everything

until he went to bed and put
his shoes outside the door.
They did get shined.

I can't remember what went—heart
or liver, or at what age.
He had thick eyelashes

(behind glasses) and a trustworthy
wit. But the phrase, the five
placed words, visit

my moon's glimpses, and certain
silences. I don't know how many
possess them.

He wrote the phrase that said
. . . The last great look of loss . . . "The last
      great
        look
          of
            loss."

Old Mr. Forrester

Old Mr. Forrester—light, light as a leaf,
Brown, dessicated, and attached by just
The thinnest stem to motion and the sun.
He sat all day in the precious, vanishing warmth,
And watched his feet in black and shining shoes,
And watched his dry, blotched, unaspiring hands,
And now and then the far heights of the mountains.
And meditated, perhaps, upon his body:
That most familiar and disobedient thing,
Which in time segments was his abject slave,
Dressed as he willed, raised, lowered, hot or cold,
But in the sweep, the arc disclosing itself,
Altering with silent mutiny each particle
The will asserted was his own: the hair,
Changing without request its original color,
The muscles, unauthorized, loosening their grip,
The teeth deserting, the eyes treacherous, and
The lazy blood
Slack in its flowing and unpunishable.
And meditated, perhaps, upon his soul—
Which meant heaven knew what—the inner thing
With which he had incuriously lived
Until the prospect of its company
On a trip into territory where this would be
Presumably the Friend to Have, the *Visé*,
The Contact, made him desire to cultivate

An alien whose speech he did not know
And the long residence of whose proximity
Might make him now a sullen and suspicious
Prospect for this belated amity.

Manny in the Wasps' Nest

Small, dark, with big spectacles and the voice of a corncrake.
He knew where he was. He kept it clean but he kept it fast.
He was the only thing moving, and there sat the solid crowd,
not so grim as they looked to him nor nearly so meaty.

It was like a truce. They laughed a little, and then more
because it was short and Manny was a comic; his dying mother-in-law
said, "Get a handsome stone . . . Not bad," and he flashed his diamond,
and they laughed indulgently as though they were free to laugh with
   him.

He came by an error, but he was there to give and they to receive,
      and it was a kind of truce.
He told a joke, did a trick with the diamond ring, told a joke:
his mother-in-law said, "What's this fly doing in my soup?"
I said to her, "I think it's the breast stroke."

He set fire to a guest's handkerchief, but it turned out whole,
      as did the cut rope—
("Nothing gets destroyed," said Manny, "nobody gets embarrassed. . . .")
He played a flute shaped like a toilet-plunger, and a snake
rose jerkily out of a basket with a scarf in its mouth.

They met on formal terms: his laughter. It was a sort of truce by chance.
All chasms, baskets; all snakes, stuffed, with jewels to return;
(no one embarrassed; nothing gets destroyed).
Small, dark, and different on the point of a needle.
      At the end, "God bless you," said Manny, "and let's dance."

Baseball as Etiquette

Baseball is etiquette made beautiful.
A quality pitch is fact, not rumor;
style is high. Do they say to the dangerous batter
who has walked, "Joe, take first?" Never, never.
The catcher, tall as fate, looms over,
his mammoth hand held high,
and the ball thunks his glove in perfect logic,
before the batter tosses his bat.
And when a batter trots back to triumphant home,
does he get his high-fives only from those
with whom he has a beer?
His worst enemy, if he has one,
is perfect in ritual; even in home glory
the pattern holds until the park
is emptied of the ball.
The famous three—movement, velocity, location—
are sacred and do not bow.
When the dark takes the diamond
and the unforgiving brown circle of loneliness,
a covenant has been confirmed.

The Companions

Living close to death
is not just a case of breath after breath.
It is to realize that to fraternize
with the dark prince is possible and wise,
so that in the final weather
when together you quit the room
though tentative and weary
you will have the enormous answer
to the enormous query.

Obit

The lovely lady posted in red,
No Hunting. Last night
the supreme hunter crossed the meadow,
into the house, to the target.

Voyage

Off sand at the edge of bush the ribs
of a fisherman's intentions spring
toward the sea; the old sea shape

stained by rains, gnawed by beach rats,
a copybook illustration, "Aspiration
Versus Attainment." There by the sound of water

the hoarse talk of water, suck and hiss,
this marine intention
more the sea's creature

than that hotel the fathoms float.
Sand's grainy grip tightens
and foliage takes back its wood.

What of the fisherman?
Did he reach the blue glitter?
Are his fingers bone?

The vines are coming.
The vines are coming.
A tendril has touched the keel.

RECENTLY DISCOVERED POEMS
FROM THE
1930s AND 1940s

Purgatory Is Nearer in November

November is beautiful as the word sounds, is gray, is bare,
Is compact of wind, of leaves blown and the thin, tall rain;
Brought back to our care are the dead in November,
and the air of these days is charged with their pain.

For these are not the free dead, not the remote, bright crowd
Of our picture-book, or our image of nebulous heaven:
These are caught, tangled in a web comfortless as a shroud—
These have not familiar place, nor flight, nor oblivion, even.

They have not escaped yet—they are close in the clouds massing
    together;
At the cold first drop you will stare on the dark ground and remember.
They are the accent of autumn, they are the source of the tone of this
    weather.
The heart is reached by the waiting dead, in their month, in November.

Boy and Girl in November

Today there is a mist on the sun and the leaves remember
The warm June winds and the bees' midsummer sound,
Earth flexes her back to meet the foot of November
Striding in chill over the hardened ground.

A boy and a girl have paused in the autumn weather,
Meeting by luck in the thin and muted sun;
Saying that there is frost, they have drawn together,
Laughing, and saying that winter is just begun;

Saying that winter is here, but without belief
That winter is more than snow. And beneath their words
And their tentative gaze, lies the bough that is breaking to leaf,
And the pointing of scarlet bud, and the stir of birds.

Natural

Clem Carver lived with his mother down by the tracks
  where the trains went by
Shaking the house, with a rush and a bell by day
  and a glare and rush in the night;
Wherever she went, he stumped at her side;
  if she left him an instant, he'd cry,
And even with her, his thick man's face was sick
  as a child's in fright.

We used to wonder sometimes what he would do,
  when, in his little room
At February dusk, or on a still August night,
  he found she was gone for good?
In what direction his big white face would turn
  and seek, to whom
He could tell the urgent, unspoken things that she
  in some part understood.

(Typed ms. copy is dated "New England – 1941")

25

Parrot

"Get along pal!" the parrot mutters.
This is the sole remark he utters,
Yet visitors delight in it
As evidence of mother-wit,
Crying, "Imagine such acumen!
One would believe the thing was human!"
In admiration at this ghost
Of talk from a creature who has lost
The lovely rapid speech of birds,
To croak three embryonic words.

Obscurity

Our loverhood is as a house, unlit,
Wherein we hunt. It has no rooted rooms
Nor is there any helpful light in it
To succor us, uncertain in its glooms.
We are compeers in doubt. On some dim stairs
I move while you are down some changeful hall;
Or if we snatch a glimpse, to our despairs, —
A freak of face by taper—: worst of all
To know our closeness and yet, miss the touch,
Yet, find our candle quenched in dark, again
Catch but cold shadows in our house of night
From faintly silvered mirrors. Yet this much
We have to cherish courage: moments when
We have encountered naked in the light.

Recruit, On the Hill

These folk on the hill, under the whisper of grass,
Were familiar; we knew the voice and the friendly face.
They cannot be alien to us, though come to this pass,
They are stock of our stock, we can trust them, though removed
   to this place.

So a brown young man, in July, in the soundless sunshine of noon,
Come before leaving to visit where these stay,
Aware that he may not return, and knowing that soon
This will be lost to his senses as yesterday,

Might steady himself, might silently stand and borrow
The knowledge here; might find these can dismiss
The strange and terrible shape of his reeling tomorrow,
On the hill, in the summer sun, as simply as this:

There is never more to say than, "We had to go;
To quit the colors, the sounds, the scents; we could not wait.
Not even for love." There is no more to know
Than this old word, no other loss, no stricter gate.

(Ms. copy includes date: "New England – 1941")

Color Song

(from *The Queen's Songs*)

God gave us different colors, she said,
That burn in the world alway,
And some, she said, show best by night,
And some by day.

White lieth the dust upon the road
And moons, when they are new,
Be white, and the shroud that a woman sewed
May well be, too.

Red is the tip of the sharp green bud
Where the small bright roses grow
In the August sun, and fresh-spilled blood
Is red also.

In the new-come dawn a pallid blue
Be skies above the ships
Of the fishing folk, and the same is true
Of a dead man's lips.

Green be the eyes of beasts by dark,
And bits of broken glass,
Green grows the moss on the forest-bark,
But greenest is grave-grass.

The Author

Josephine Jacobsen was born August 19, 1908, in Coburg, Canada, to American parents. She began writing poetry as a child, and, at the age of ten, saw her first work published in *St. Nicholas Magazine*. Major recognition did not come until 1971 when, at the age of sixty-three, she was named Consultant in Poetry to the Library of Congress. Over the course of a long and distinguished career, she published nine collections of poetry, four collections of short fiction, a volume of occasional pieces, and two volumes of criticism (the last co-authored with William R. Mueller). Her life's work in poetry is collected in *In the Crevice of Time: New and Collected Poems* (Johns Hopkins Press, 1995).

In the last fifteen years of her life, Jacobsen received the Lenore Marshall Poetry Prize, the annual fellowship from the Academy of American Poets, the Shelley Memorial Award, the Poets' Prize, and the Robert Frost Medal, the Poetry Society of America's highest honor, given for lifetime achievement. A member of the American Academy of Arts and Letters, and a regular contributor to *The New Yorker*, she lived in Baltimore, Maryland, for many years with her husband Eric Jacobsen. She died July 9, 2003.

Works by Josephine Jacobsen

Poetry

Let Each Man Remember (1940)
For the Unlost (1946)
The Human Climate (1953)
The Animal Inside (1966)
The Shade-Seller (1974)
The Chinese Insomniacs (1981)
The Sisters (1987)
Distances (1991)
In the Crevice of Time (1995)

Fiction

A Walk With Rashid (1979)
Adios, Mr. Moxley (1986)
On the Island (1989)
What Goes Without Saying (1996)

Nonfiction

*The Instant of Knowing: Lectures, Criticism and
    Occasional Prose*, edited by Elizabeth Spires (1997)

Criticism (co-authored with William R. Mueller):

Genet and Ionesco: Playwrights of Silence (1968)
The Testament of Samuel Beckett (1964)